WONDERS OF CANADA

The Historic District of Old-Quebec

Leia Tait

Weigl
CALGARY
www.weigl.com

Published by Weigl Educational Publishers Limited
6325 10th Street SE
Calgary, Alberta
T2H 2Z9

Website: www.weigl.com

We acknowledge the financial support of the Government of Canada through the Book Publishing Industry Development Program (BPIDP) for our publishing activities.

Library and Archives Canada Cataloguing in Publication

Tait, Leia
The Historic District of Old-Quebec / Leia Tait.

(Wonders of Canada)
Includes index.
ISBN 978-1-55388-393-7 (bound)
ISBN 978-1-55388-394-4 (pbk.)

1. Vieux-Québec (Québec, Québec)--Juvenile literature. 2. World heritage areas--Québec (Province)--Québec--Juvenile literature.
I. Title. II. Series.
FC2946.33.T35 2007 j971.4'471 C2007-902260-X

Printed in the United States of America
1 2 3 4 5 6 7 8 9 0 11 10 09 08 07

Photograph Credits

Every reasonable effort has been made to trace ownership and to obtain permission to reprint copyright material. The publishers would be pleased to have any errors or omissions brought to their attention so that they may be corrected in subsequent printings.

Library and Archives Canada: page 11 left (PA-028628)

Project Coordinator
Leia Tait

Design
Terry Paulhus

Contents

City of History, City of Culture

Imagine a city centuries older than Canada. Thick, stone walls surround the city. Horse-drawn carriages roll down cobblestone streets. Musicians play on street corners. Churches crowd the skyline.

This is the Historic District of Old-Quebec. It is the heart of Quebec City, one of the oldest cities in Canada. It is also the only walled city north of Mexico. Many of the buildings in the Historic District were built before 1850. Some have stood for 400 years.

The Historic District of Old-Quebec is the birthplace of French **culture** in North America. It is also a visual wonder, with stunning natural scenery, handsome buildings, and a vibrant atmosphere. The area is alive with history and culture. The Historic District of Old-Quebec became a World Heritage Site in 1985.

Horse-drawn carriages, called *caléches*, are common in the Historic District of Old-Quebec.

What is a World Heritage Site?

Heritage is what people inherit from those who lived before them. It is also what they pass down to future generations. Heritage is made up of many things. Objects, traditions, beliefs, values, places, and people are all part of heritage. Throughout history, these things have been **preserved**. A family's heritage is preserved in the stories, customs, and objects its members pass on to each other. Similarly, a common human heritage is preserved in the beliefs, objects, and places that have special meaning for all people, such as the Historic District of Old-Quebec.

The United Nations Educational, Scientific and Cultural Organization (UNESCO) identifies places around the world that are important to all people. Some are important places in nature. Others are related to culture. These landmarks become World Heritage Sites. They are protected from being destroyed by **urbanization,** pollution, tourism, and neglect.

A funicular, or type of cable railway, shuttles visitors between different parts of the Historic District of Old-Quebec.

You can learn more about UNESCO World Heritage Sites by visiting **http://whc.unesco.org.**

Think about it

World Heritage Sites belong to all people. They provide a link to the past. These sites also help people from many cultures connect with each other. Think about your own heritage. What landmarks are important to you? Think about the places that have shaped your life. Make a list of your personal heritage sites. The list might include your home, your grandparents' home, your school, or any other place that is special to you and your family. Next to each location on the list, write down why it is important to you.

Where in the World?

Quebec City is the capital of the province of Quebec. The city is located in southern Quebec. It sits on a cliff overlooking the St. Lawrence River. The Historic District of Old-Quebec is the oldest part of the city. It covers 135 hectares. This is about 5 percent of the city's total area.

The Historic District is made up of two sections. They are called Upper Town and Lower Town. Upper Town sits on top of the cliff. It overlooks the river. Upper Town is home to many government offices, churches, and military buildings. Lower Town is located at the foot of the cliff. It lies along the riverbank. Here, houses with steep, colourful roofs line the narrow streets. Many shops can also be found in this area. A steep staircase, called *L'Escalier Casse-Cou*, or "Breakneck Staircase," links Lower Town and Upper Town. An elevator-like funicular also provides travel between the two zones.

Quebec's dramatic skyline is one reason why many people believe the city is among the most beautiful in the world.

Puzzler

"Quebec" comes from the **Aboriginal** word *kebec*, meaning "where the river narrows." It was given this name because, at Quebec City, the St. Lawrence River narrows to a width of about 1 kilometre. Other places in the province of Quebec are also named for their natural features. Using the translations, match the Quebec place names below to the numbers on the map.

ANSWERS: 1. D, 2. B, 3. E, 4. A, 5. C

N W E S
Scale 0 125 Kilometres
QUEBEC
Gulf of St. Lawrence
D
C
B
NEW BRUNSWICK
E
A
UNITED STATES OF AMERICA
ONTARIO

1. Chibougamu
Aboriginal name meaning "where the water is shut in"

2. Gaspé
Aboriginal name meaning "land's end"

3. Quebec City
French name meaning "where the river narrows"

4. Montreal
French name meaning "mount royal"

5. Saguenay
Aboriginal name meaning "where the water flows out"

A Trip Back in Time

For thousands of years, Aboriginal Peoples occupied the site of what is now Quebec City. French explorers first visited the spot in 1535. They did not return until 1608, when explorer Samuel de Champlain travelled up the St. Lawrence River. Champlain built a fort on the riverbank under some cliffs. He called the fort Quebec. The fort stood at the site of present-day Lower Town. Later, Champlain built another fort on top of the cliffs. This was Château St-Louis. It was the beginning of present-day Upper Town.

Quebec quickly became the French capital of North America. Settlers built schools, churches, and hospitals. They also built **fortifications** to protect the settlement from British attacks. For more than 150 years, France and Great Britain fought for control of North America. In 1759, the British army took control of Quebec. Within a few years, they controlled all of France's land in North America. Under British control, Quebec grew into a strong, **military** city. By the mid-1800s, it was home to more than 42,000 people.

Champlain made a drawing of Quebec in 1613. The fort had two main dwellings, a storehouse, a watchtower, cannon platforms, and gardens.

Site Science

For protection, the French built fortifications in and around the settlement at Quebec. They built wooden walls around the city and placed cannons on the walls overlooking the St. Lawrence River. When the British took control of the city, they expanded the fortifications. The British strengthened the walls with slabs of thick stone. They also built large circular towers, called Martello towers, around the outside of the city. The greatest part of the British defence works was the Citadel. This was a massive, stone fortress built at the top of the cliff. The star-shaped structure took more than 10 years to build. It made Quebec a true military city.

The St. Louis gate in Upper Town is one of the main gates leading into the Historic District of Old-Quebec. Many guided tours of the fortifications begin here.

FIND MORE ONLINE

Tour Quebec's fortifications by clicking on "3D Tour" at **www.pc.gc.ca/lhn-nhs/qc/fortifications/index_e.asp.** Click on the tour highlights along the left side of the page.

Becoming a World Heritage Site

Quebec City grew rapidly during the 1800s. By the 1850s, the city had outgrown its walls. Many people wanted to tear down the fortifications to make room for the city to grow. **Governor General** Lord Frederick Dufferin stopped this from happening. In the 1870s, he convinced city leaders to preserve Quebec's walls and other historic buildings. A century later, the fortifications were completely **restored**.

In 1983, city leaders suggested that the Historic District of Old-Quebec be recognized as a World Heritage Site. They pointed out that Quebec is the only walled city in North America with well-preserved fortifications. Few cities in North America have buildings older than 150 years. They noted that the Historic District is the source of French culture in North America. It is a key location in French, British, and Canadian history. As a result, UNESCO declared the Historic District of Old-Quebec a World Heritage Site in 1985.

Quebec was the first city in North America to become a World Heritage Site.

Heritage Heroes

Lord Frederick Dufferin was a member of the British government. His full title was Lord Frederick Temple Blackwood, 1st Marquess of Dufferin and Ava. Dufferin became Canada's governor general in 1872. At the time, Great Britain had a great deal of control over Canada. Lord Dufferin worked to ensure that Canada's laws and policies agreed with those of Great Britain.

As governor general, Dufferin travelled to each province. He often stated how much he enjoyed Quebec City. In 1872, Dufferin made a second home for his family at the Citadel. When city officials wanted to take down the city walls, Dufferin opposed. He believed the fortifications were an important part of Canada's heritage.

Dufferin convinced the Canadian government to preserve the walls and other historic landmarks in Quebec. He provided some of his own money for these projects. Lord Dufferin also designed a walkway to be added to the Citadel. In 1878, Dufferin's last public act as governor general was to lay the first stone in the walkway. It was named Dufferin Terrace in his honour.

Today, Dufferin Terrace stretches from the Citadel to the Château Frontenac. It is one of the most visited spots in the city.

World Heritage in CANADA

There are more than 800 UNESCO World Heritage Sites in 138 countries around the globe. Canada has 14 of these sites. Seven are natural sites, and seven are cultural sites. Each is believed to be of outstanding heritage value to all people around the world. Look at the map. Are any of these sites near your home? Have you visited any of them? Learn more about World Heritage Sites in Canada by visiting www.pc.gc.ca/progs/spm-whs/itm2-/index_e.asp.

Canadian Rocky Mountain Parks (Alberta and British Columbia)

- A mountain landscape created by North America's largest mountain range
- Home of the Burgess Shale **fossil** site, one of the world's most important collections of **prehistoric** marine fossils

Dinosaur Provincial Park (Alberta)

- One of the largest and most important collections of dinosaur fossils in the world

Gros Morne National Park (Newfoundland)

- The site of spectacular scenery created by movement in Earth's crust and the uncovering of ancient rocks

1. Canadian Rocky Mountain Parks (Alberta and British Columbia)
2. Dinosaur Provincial Park (Alberta)
3. Gros Morne National Park (Newfoundland and Labrador)
4. Head-Smashed-In Buffalo Jump (Alberta)

5 The Historic District of Old-Quebec (Quebec)

6 Kluane/Wrangell-St Elias/Glacier Bay/Tatshenshini-Alsek (British Columbia, Yukon, and Alaska)

7 L'Anse aux Meadows National Historic Site (Newfoundland and Labrador)

8 Miguasha National Park (Quebec)

9 Nahanni National Park Reserve (Northwest Territories)

10 Old Town Lunenburg (Nova Scotia)

11 Rideau Canal (Ontario)

12 SGang Gwaay (British Columbia)

13 Waterton Glacier International Peace Park (Alberta and Montana)

14 Wood Buffalo National Park (Alberta and Northwest Territories)

Natural Wonders

The Historic District of Old-Quebec is known for its striking landscape. The St. Lawrence River flows past Lower Town. The river was formed 10,000 years ago by melting **glaciers.** It stretches from the Atlantic Ocean to the interior of North America. European explorers first found the river in 1535. For centuries, it was the main route for exploration, trade, and settlement in North America. Today, the St. Lawrence is used as a shipping route. It remains the most important waterway in Canada, and is often called the "Great River of Canada." Many animals, including whales, raccoons, beavers, and birds, make their homes in or near the river.

At Quebec City, the St. Lawrence narrows around a massive, grey cliff called *Cap Diamant*, or "Cape Diamond." The cliff towers about 100 metres above the river. Cap Diamant is the site of Upper Town in the Historic District of Old-Quebec.

At 1,200 kilometres, the St. Lawrence River is one of the longest rivers in North America.

FIND MORE ONLINE

Learn more about the St. Lawrence River by visiting **www.thecanadianencyclopedia.com** and typing "*St. Lawrence River*" into the search box.

Creature Feature

The beaver is a large, furry **rodent**. It has reddish-brown fur, a large, flat tail, and powerful teeth. Beavers can swim well. Using sticks, roots, mud, and rocks, they build dams in forest streams. The dams create shallow ponds, where beavers build their homes, called lodges. Beavers are one of the few animals that can change their **habitat** in this way.

The beaver is one of the most important animals in Canadian history. In the late 1500s, hats made from beaver fur became popular in Europe. Explorers of what is now Canada found the land rich in beaver. They began trading with Aboriginal Peoples, supplying European goods in return for beaver furs. Trading posts, like the one Champlain built at Quebec, made it easier for these two groups to trade. For 250 years, the fur trade was Canada's most important industry. It helped shape the country.

At the peak of the fur trade, nearly 100,000 beaver furs were shipped from Canada to Europe each year.

Cultural Treasures

The Historic District of Old-Quebec was home to the first permanent settlers in Canada. Most of these settlers came from France. They spoke French and practised European traditions. Over time, these settlers created their own French-Canadian culture. Today, this culture thrives in the Historic District of Old-Quebec. Tourists travel from all over the world to experience the area's food, fine art, music, and theatre.

About 5,000 people live in the Historic District of Old-Quebec. This is about one percent of Quebec City's entire population. Residents in the Historic District are a mix of students, politicians, nuns, priests, shopkeepers, artists, musicians, soldiers, and sailors. They share their unique culture and history with the many visitors to their special city.

The New France Festival takes place in the Historic District each August. More than 9,000 people celebrate French heritage with music, dancing, food, and costumes.

Telling Tales

Stories are an important part of French-Canadian culture. Ti-Jean, or "Little John," is a character in many French-Canadian tales. One well-known story is called "Ti-Jean and the Big White Cat."

There was once a king who had three sons. One of them was named Ti-Jean. The king gave his sons three tests to see who should be king after him. First, he sent them to find the best horse. They each took a different path through the forest.

Ti-Jean came to a cottage with a big white cat. He told the cat about the horse. "Take one of my toads," said the cat. "When you get back to the palace, it will become a fine horse." Ti-Jean took the toad. It became the best horse his father had ever seen.

Next, the king sent his sons to find the most beautiful piece of cloth. Ti-Jean returned to the big white cat. "Take one of my walnuts," she said. "You will find a cloth inside." Ti-Jean took the walnut back to the palace. When he cracked it open, the fine cloth inside impressed the king again.

Finally, the king said whoever found the most beautiful girl would be the next king. Ti-Jean found the white cat again. "I have a spell on me," she explained. "When I marry a prince, I shall become a woman once more." She returned to the palace with Ti-Jean. When they were married, the cat turned into the loveliest woman in the land. Ti-Jean became king.

Amazing Attractions

The Historic District of Old-Quebec is best explored on foot. There are many historical treasures for visitors to discover. Lower Town is home to the oldest buildings in the city. Place-Royale, a cobblestone square, is located at the place where Champlain's fort stood 400 years ago. Traditional displays of music and dance are often performed in the square. Museums, art galleries, restaurants, and shops surround Place-Royale.

Many churches and religious buildings are found in Upper Town. North America's oldest school for girls is the Ursuline **Convent**. It was built in 1639. That same year, a group of nuns established Hôtel-Dieu. This was the first hospital in Canada. The Cathedral of Notre Dame was built in 1647. It has been destroyed by fire and rebuilt three times since it was first built.

The Church of Notre-Dame-des-Victoires was built in the 1680s. It stands on the site of Samuel de Champlain's first residence, on the Place-Royale in Lower Town.

Featured Attraction

The Château Frontenac is Quebec City's best-known landmark. This 618-room hotel towers over Upper Town, on what was once the site of Champlain's Château St-Louis.

The Canadian Pacific Railway built the Château Frontenac in 1893. It looks like the castles that are found in France. Steep roofs and rounded towers decorate each building of the hotel. Visitors to the Historic District can stay at the hotel or take a guided tour inside the richly decorated building.

KEY ISSUES

Issues in Heritage

The Historic District of Old-Quebec is a small part of a large, modern city. As Quebec City grows, the Historic District is threatened by urbanization. More and more people are moving to the area. Houses, buildings, schools, and malls are being built. City planners work hard to meet the needs of people who live there while preventing Quebec's heritage from being lost. To do this, they focus on preserving the most important buildings in Old-Quebec, instead of trying to save everything.

The great number of visitors is another problem in the Historic District of Old-Quebec. More than 5.3 million tourists visit the site each year. This is a very large number of people for a small area. Crowding can ruin the historic feeling of the site. Tourists may also damage the historic buildings and put stress on local services.

Tour buses bringing loads of visitors to the Historic District are a particular problem in the Historic District of Old-Quebec. They cause traffic jams and make air and noise pollution. People who live in the area work together with city planners to better manage this problem.

Cars are only allowed on certain streets in the Historic District.

FIND MORE ONLINE

Learn more about Quebec City at **www.ville.quebec.qc.ca/en.**

Should tourist buses be allowed in the Historic District of Old-Quebec?

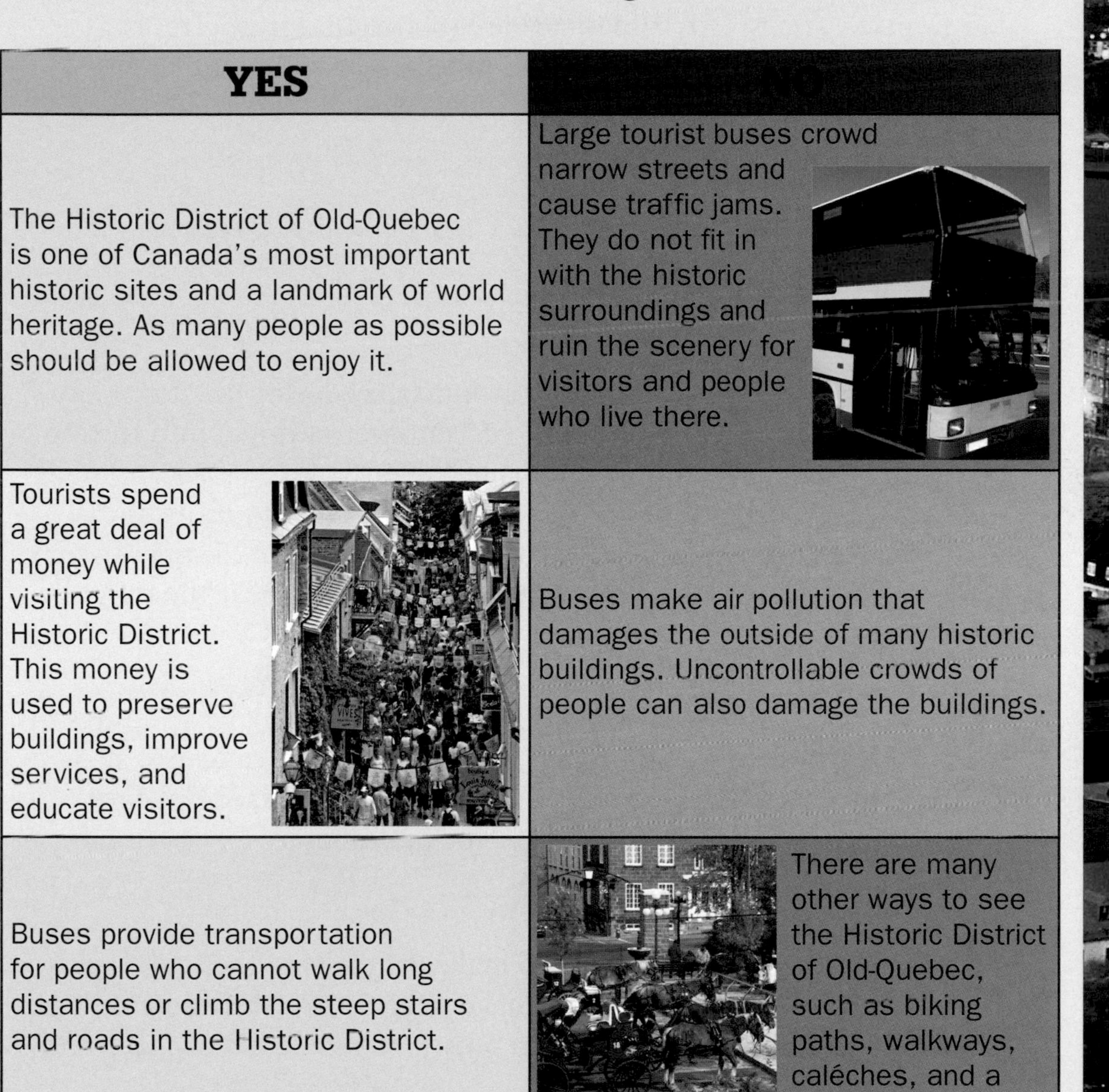

YES	NO
The Historic District of Old-Quebec is one of Canada's most important historic sites and a landmark of world heritage. As many people as possible should be allowed to enjoy it.	Large tourist buses crowd narrow streets and cause traffic jams. They do not fit in with the historic surroundings and ruin the scenery for visitors and people who live there.
Tourists spend a great deal of money while visiting the Historic District. This money is used to preserve buildings, improve services, and educate visitors.	Buses make air pollution that damages the outside of many historic buildings. Uncontrollable crowds of people can also damage the buildings.
Buses provide transportation for people who cannot walk long distances or climb the steep stairs and roads in the Historic District.	There are many other ways to see the Historic District of Old-Quebec, such as biking paths, walkways, calèches, and a funicular elevator.

Think about this issue. Are there any possible solutions that would satisfy both sides of the debate?

Build a Fortified Settlement

Materials Needed

125 popsicle sticks, 1 styrofoam square (about 15 centimetres by 30 centimetres), coloured construction paper, brown paint, green paint, glue

Paint 70 popsicle sticks brown. Then, paint the styrofoam base green.

Leave a 2.5-centimetre border around the edge of the styrofoam. Push the popsicle sticks about 2.5 centimetres down into the top of the styrofoam to build the walls of the fort. Use 28 sticks to build the first wall along a long side of the base. With 14 more sticks, build each of the shorter side walls. Use the other 25 sticks to make the final front wall. Leave an opening for a gate near the centre.

Use the remaining unpainted popsicle sticks to make buildings inside the fort. Your buildings can include living quarters, a storehouse, a chapel, a kitchen, and a blacksmith forge. Leave room for a courtyard in front of the buildings.

Cut brown paper rectangles to make the roofs of the buildings. Fold the rectangles in half to make steep roofs. Glue them on top of the building walls. Cut out a brown rectangle for the gate, and then glue it to the fort walls.

Make other features, such as a flag, a vegetable garden, or a well, from construction paper. Add these items to the fort.

Quiz

1. Who founded Quebec City?
2. What is the name of Canada's first hospital?
3. True or false? The otter had an important impact on the history of Quebec City.
4. How many tourists visit the Historic District of Old-Quebec each year?
   a. 1 million b. 3.5 million c. 5.3 million d. 10 million
5. Where are the oldest buildings in the Historic District located?

ANSWERS: 1. Samuel de Champlain 2. Hôtel-Dieu 3. False. The beaver was important in Quebec City's history. 4. c. 5.3 million 5. Place-Royale in Lower Town

Further Research

You can find more information about the Historic District of Old-Quebec at your local library or on the Internet.

Libraries

Most libraries have computers that connect to a database for researching information. If you input a key word, you will be provided with a list of books in the library that contain information on that topic. Non-fiction books are arranged numerically, using their call number. Fiction books are organized alphabetically by the author's last name.

Websites

Explore Champlain's early Quebec settlement at **www.civilization.ca/vmnf/expos/champlain/bat2_eng.html.**

Join the UNESCO World Heritage in Young Hands Project for students at **http://whc.unesco.org/education.**

Glossary

Aboriginal: related to Aboriginal Peoples, who are the first people who lived in Canada and their descendants, including First Nations, Inuit, and Métis

convent: a building where nuns live

culture: the characteristics, beliefs, and practices of a racial, religious, or social group

fortifications: constructions built for defence

fossil: the remains or traces of living things preserved in earth or rock

glaciers: massive, slow-moving bodies of ice

governor general: a government official who represents the British crown in Canada

habitat: the place where a plant or animal naturally lives or grows

military: having to do with the armed forces, soldiers, or war

prehistoric: belonging to the period before written history

preserved: protected from injury, loss, or ruin

restored: brought back to its original state

rodent: a small type of warm-blooded animal that has sharp front teeth used for gnawing

urbanization: the movement of people out of the countryside and into cities

Index